Contents

Foreword

High/Scope offers two vitally important ingredients to anyone who is concerned about the quality of the curriculum in its widest sense in nursery classes and day nurseries. First, it is based on a multi-disciplinary approach to training which enables teachers, nursery nurses, advisers and other professionals to participate together. Second, it provides a coherent common framework within the nursery in which all staff can work together as equal partners to provide an enriching experience for the children.

VOLCUF has been promoting an interest in the High/Scope approach in the UK throughout the 1980s, organising seminars at which David Weikart, Director of the High/Scope Educational Trust, presented an account of his innovative work in the USA. Between 1984 and 1989 a development worker was employed by VOLCUF to carry out a High/Scope training programme. This work was funded by the Aga Khan Foundation, Barnardos, the Gulbenkian Foundation and others.

A High/Scope Institute is now to be established to continue and expand this work. For further information, contact The High/Scope Institute, c/o Research and Development Section, Barnardos, Tanners Lane, Barkingside, Essex IG6 1QG.

Audrey Langdown, a nursery teacher in the north east of England, attended a VOLCUF seminar at which her imagination was captured by the High/Scope approach. VOLCUF was delighted to receive this engaging 'warts-and-all' account of her work and to have the opportunity of publishing it.

Judith Stone
VOLCUF General Secretary
July 1989

GETTING STARTED

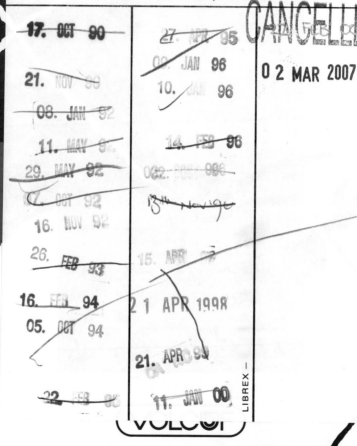

:336/
6.00

This book is to be returned on or before
the last date stamped below.

CoL·B 43361 /6· 11·89

Published by
VOLCUF
77 Holloway Road
London N7 8JZ

Tel: 01-607 9573

VOLCUF is a registered charity which aims to support and enhance the work of voluntary groups in promoting and developing improvements in services for children under five and their families. VOLCUF provides information and support, organises a programme of training, promotes good practice and acts as an advocate on behalf of the voluntary sector.

ISBN 1 870 985 06 0

Introduction

A recipe can be unique without having any unfamiliar ingredients. The comprehensive curriculum developed by the High/Scope Education Research Foundation in the United States is such a 'recipe'. In 1983 I listened to a lecture given by High/Scope's founding director, David Weikart, and decided to begin a project introducing High/Scope to the nursery class where I worked in the North of England.

After working with nursery aged children for seven years it had become increasingly obvious to me that my own practice needed to be revitalised, and issues such as parental involvement, team management and so on should be reassessed. I also needed to observe more closely what the children were *actually doing* during their time in the nursery.

I commenced a course of part-time study, where my main option was 'Education Management'. This proved to be a vital source of information and ideas concerning organisational change, particularly as I felt that a re-examination of past practices and current problems was essential before the introduction of a new curriculum. This book is based on action research carried out for my coursework and dissertation, and it has been edited to make it available to a wider audience.

In the school which is the focus of this study the development of the High/Scope curriculum was welcomed, the underlying assumption being that it would improve both staff and pupil performance. High/Scope was chosen because its emphasis on a team approach and parental involvement made it a curriculum which seemed ideal for pre-school children in an educational priority area.

During this project, crucial issues were raised regarding professionalism, nursery nurse/teacher roles, curriculum planning, school management, the assessment and diagnosis of children's needs and educational practice. I also needed to identify ways of working with all the adults in the nursery as equal partners. Additionally, the traditional role of nursery teacher (myself) had to be redefined.

Recent research into professional roles identifies some of the possible demands made of a nursery teacher:

☐ the teacher may have to act as a catalyst, enabler, supporter, partner, outreach worker and counsellor;

☐ the teacher may have to learn new skills such as self awareness, listening, jargon-free communication, team work and a non-judgemental approach;

☐ the teacher may experience a new vulnerability, e.g. personal rejection, personal criticism, independent and assertive staff;

- [ ] the teacher may have to act as development, diagnostic and interpretive adviser, problem defining and problem clarifying;

- [ ] the teacher may have to train staff to observe, record and teach;

- [ ] the teacher will need support, resources, training and time.

It is with the knowledge of these factors, and bearing them in mind, that this study has been undertaken.

Chapter one

Nursery education

In order to understand the framework for this study, it is necessary to comment upon the educational trends that have influenced Local Education Authorities and the school, following publication of the Plowden report *Children and their Primary Schools* in 1967.

National and international trends in education

The Plowden report recommended compensatory education for disadvantaged children. Extra resources were given to schools in underprivileged areas to compensate for disadvantages the children were thought to have suffered in their pre-school years. The school where my research took place was in a social priority area, and a nursery class was opened in 1971.

Although it has been stressed in recent years that the goals of provision for the under-fives should be the present well-being and development of all young children and their families, irrespective of long-term benefits, such services in both Britain and the United States were expanded in the belief that they were particularly valuable for children whose home environment was restricted. The concept of disadvantage and the difficulty of assessing pre-school programmes have both been extensively debated.[1]

The Westinghouse critique and other evaluations of the Head Start Project in America showed that after three years in school the benefits of compensatory pre-school programmes had faded. A similar pattern emerges from United Kingdom studies of the long term effectiveness of nursery education. [2] However, more recent studies in both countries have yielded more optimistic results, particularly with respect to 'sleeper' effects which may only emerge in the long term. [3]

One of the best designed of these longitudinal studies was carried out by David Weikart and his colleagues in Ypsilanti, Michigan, beginning in the 1960's. They followed the progress of two groups of disadvantaged children, one of which attended a pre-school programme now known as High/Scope, and another group who entered school without attending pre-school of any kind. The most recent report on this study is *Changed Lives* (High/Scope Press, 1984) which illustrates how pre-school education can produce enormous educational, social and economic gains, indicating that both individual and public commitment to early education is extremely important. For over twenty years two groups of children were followed from age three to young adulthood. When both groups were compared it was found that those with pre-school education had:

1 – better school achievement

2 – higher high-school graduation and college attendance rates

3 – lower juvenile delinquency and adult crime rates

4 – less welfare dependency

5 – less teenage pregnancy and lower childbearing rates

6 – increased rates of job-holding and job-training.

These observations have enormous social implications for us as educators and for society at large, showing how nursery education can have strong practical benefits. In fact, American policy-makers have been so heartened by the long-term financial benefits of pre-school that they have expanded early education programmes, especially for disadvantaged children, throughout the United States. *(4)*

British pre-school provision is characterised by diversity, with considerable differences in policy and objectives between different sectors. There is also considerable diversity in practice: for example, in the emphasis on different types of activity and equipment for children and in the way activities are organised for children to choose their own play or to be guided by adults; in the style and amount of interaction between adults and children; and in the attitude to parental involvement.*(5)*

Studies of early childhood and pre-school work in Britain have stressed the need for a curriculum and are critical of the content of provision. Barbara Tizard and Jerome Bruner*(6)* made serious criticisms of the traditional British 'free play' curriculum. After studying provision in a variety of pre school settings Bruner says:

> One gets the impression, observing nursery schools and playgroups, that they are often unclear and at a cross purpose about what they are trying to do. They attempt to serve so many functions that they fail to enlist to the full the growing intellectual energies and skills of the three and four year olds whom they principally serve.*(7)*

Tizard's report, confirmed by Bruner, prompted angry outcry and much debate. Slowly an informal consensus has developed concerning the need for more structured programmes, but there is little agreement on how this goal should be translated into practice. Should there be more teacher directed activities? School-readiness teaching? Many of the contentious issues have now been clarified, but the problems of pre-school programmes have not been resolved.

In the decade since Tizard's report, new initiatives have been made but these have largely focused on the *organisation* and delivery of services, and less on the *content* of the provision for either child or parent.

An additional concern when looking at curricular provision for the under fives is the increasing trend of admitting children to school at the start of the year in which they become five (revealed in a National Foundation for Education Research survey of 1983). This means that more children are entering primary school at just four years of age. The appropriate provision for younger fours in infant classes has recently attracted attention in Parliament, in the press and in several official reports (Assistant Masters and Mistresses Association, 1987 and National Foundation for Education Research/School Curriculum Development Council ,1987).

The admission of younger fours to infant classes raises a number of questions:

☐ Are appropriate nursery experiences available in the infant school?

☐ Have reception teachers had suitable training and experience in working with four year olds?

☐ Are the needs of younger children subordinated to those of older children in the same class?

Despite increasing attention being given to the needs of four year olds in school, there is still little evidence of educational theory being used to justify specific classroom activities or to establish a common methodology.

In 1986, Christine Stevenson set out to examine the challenges to, and, by implication, the constraints on, four year old children in nursery and infant classes. She discovered, through evidence based on observations collected in England over a twelve week secondment, that teachers of our young children needed to:

☐ emphasise to parents, teachers and the community that four year olds have particular needs with regard to both equipment and environment;

☐ be freed from the belief that work and play are separate, that work is important and justifiable and play is not.

She concluded that guidelines must be agreed on because the needs of the four year old were the same whether in school or in nursery and this should become the corporate responsibility of parents, playgroup personnel, nursery personnel, infant teachers and head teachers.

> One of the greatest challenges to the teacher of four year olds in school was pressure from the community to maintain a curriculum more suited to the needs of the five to six year old child.*(8)*

The nursery sector is not included in the range of National Curriculum discussion documents recently published because it is non-statutory. Nevertheless, if nursery education is to be considered as an integral part of the education system, there must be debate and discussion about the purposes and practices of this stage of education. Consideration must be given to the care and pedagogy that we offer to young children, how we offer them and how we can check that we are being successful in our practices.

As we have already mentioned, there remains a great deal of confusion over the different provision made for children under five. There is in Britain no tried and tested system of training for work with under-fives which concentrates on both the development of curriculum and educational management, and is accessible to those working at *different levels* in a range of services. The High/Scope approach meets all those important requirements.

Curriculum planning

The teacher's task is to ensure that a child's time in the nursery is worthwhile. What is worthwhile is in itself open to debate, but the statement of the aims of education found in the Warnock Report (1978) is surely very acceptable, namely: first to enlarge a child's knowledge, experience and imaginative understanding, and thus his or her awareness of moral values and capacity for enjoyment; and secondly to enable him or her to enter the world after formal education is over as an active participant in society and a responsible contributor to it.

To start to achieve these aims in the nursery the teacher must have a curriculum. Effective curriculum planning involves:

☐ a knowledge of how young children develop and learn most effectively;

☐ familiarity with materials, activities and methods that promote different types of development and learning;

☐ determining the resources available in terms of time, staff numbers and expertise, accommodation and equipment.

Any offered curriculum is influenced by the environmental setting – the experiences and messages that children receive in school. Yet what the teacher believes she is offering may not be what is being received by the child. The *received* curriculum depends on how the curriculum is offered.

The particular skill of the nursery teacher lies in getting to know about the competences of her age-group of children. In judging what young children understands, the teacher needs to know about their past experiences, and observe their use of oral language and their actions.

Any learning difficulties that children may experience may be due to a number of inter-related factors, operating within the child, his or her environment or both. The child's progress may be impeded by:

☐ physical factors, including medical maturation or neurological factors;

☐ emotional factors, affecting the level of motivation, self-image and ability to adjust to the learning situation;

☐ intellectual factors, including his or her understanding of the concepts and processes s/he is likely to encounter in pre-school education.

Environmental factors in both school and home may also be detrimental to the child's progress. Attitudes in the home and experiences there can affect language facility, level of motivation and overall readiness to learn.

Each child's genetic endowment and the environment in which s/he finds themself combine to make him or her unique. Because young children are relatively unsocialised, limited in experience and at an egocentric stage of development, their individual characteristics will be particularly noticeable. Every nursery teacher knows this and will also accept that, while the pattern of growth and development follows a universal sequence, the rate and progress of development differ for each child. It is the child's developmental stage that is significant for his or her learning rather than his or her chronological age.

Therefore if the method by which children are taught does not take into account their developmental level, their limiting circumstances and emotional needs, their progress may be impeded and the child may develop unfavourable attitudes towards learning. The High/Scope curriculum, the subject of my research, takes into account the abilities, interests and weaknesses of young children. Both generally and in the nursery which is the focus for this study, attitudes towards non-teaching staff have changed during the last few years. Where staff were once seen as benevolent providers they are now regarded as a central resource for the child's learning; a dynamic nursery, where the accent is on school-based and school focused development, is the best possible seed-bed for professional growth.

When introducing the High/Scope curriculum over a period of three years, I aimed to provide a qualitative form of involvement both for the staff and children. My assessment of its effects on all of us is included in chapter six.

Chapter two

The case for High/Scope

The High/Scope Curriculum has its origins in the district school system in Ypsilanti, Michigan USA. In the early 1960s it became clear from some local studies that a very high proportion of children from low income families were in need of special educational services because of their various difficulties at all stages in the school system. The Director of Special Services, David Weikart, and his staff explored ways of dealing with this problem. Since there was little prospect of changing the school system as such, the idea of intervening at pre-school stage was explored and in 1962 a unit was set up alongside an existing school.

There was little idea about a specific curriculum at that stage but a commitment by staff to develop exploratively. After twenty years of research, the High/Scope curriculum evolved, several major theories and ideas being incorporated into the total scheme. A major contribution comes from the work of the Swiss psychologist Jean Piaget. In the foreword of the High/Scope manual *Young Children in Action* the curriculum model is described in the following terms:

> Piagetian theory was important in determining the content of this programme. The format of the day and the general method of the teacher/child interaction, however, were rooted in the suggestion of Smilansky, an Israeli psychologist, and traditional nursery school programming. Smilansky's three part sequence of planning, working and evaluating by children became the organising principle for the daily routine and has remained so, with some modifications, to the present time.

Thanks to Graham Oakes (Barnardo's North East Division), High/Scope's underlying theory may be summarised in the following diagram:

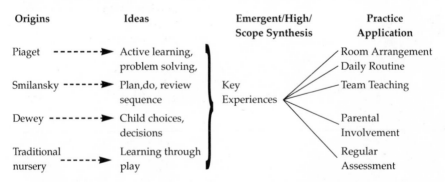

Origins	Ideas	Emergent/High/Scope Synthesis	Practice Application
Piaget	Active learning, problem solving,		Room Arrangement / Daily Routine
Smilansky	Plan, do, review sequence	Key Experiences	Team Teaching
Dewey	Child choices, decisions		Parental Involvement
Traditional nursery	Learning through play		Regular Assessment

The High/Scope Foundation assume that 'active learning – the direct and immediate experience of objects, people and events is a necessary condition for cognitive restructuring and hence for development'. Although focus on active learning makes High/Scope similar to other pre-school methods, its emphasis on a detailed set of 'key experiences' (described further in chapter 5 and the appendices) as well as daily planning by each child, is a radical departure from most other pre-school curricula. These generally focus on one of two extremes: the 'free play' methods which give children free rein to roam in a rich environment with little adult intervention, or, alternatively, methods that surround them with adult talk or instructions.

The High/Scope curriculum is based on a 'problem-solving' approach to children's learning. It also emphasises team planning, frequent evaluation, parent involvement and effective staff management.(1) Staff assess each child's stage of development and plan appropriate experiences to help the child to:

- ☐ assume responsibility

- ☐ take initiatives

- ☐ be creative

- ☐ make plans

- ☐ solve problems.

In the High/Scope classroom, children are encouraged to help make deliberate choices about their activities, to carry out their own plans, and then to discuss the outcome with adults and peers. This is achieved by having a 'planning time' each day with a group of eight or nine children. The children talk about projects and activities they wish to engage in. They decide what materials they will need and how to go about the work they have set for themselves. The staff are provided with planning boards in order to collect data about the children's plans. Adults guide play but do not dominate it; they perform what Bruner (2) calls 'scaffolding' by giving encouragement when problems arise, making suggestions when children run out of steam, and using language to transform overt actions into thought.

In each session every child participates in a cycle of 'plan-do-review'. In this cycle adults help each child to choose what to do, to carry out plans, and then to reflect on why some things went right and others went wrong.

The 'review' part of the cycle helps children to focus on their activities and see how they can develop and expand on what they have done. Reviewing is also a social experience which enables the children to join together in evaluating their work, and this increases their self-esteem.

The basic daily routine consists of distinct periods for different kinds of individual and group experiences. A typical half day programme is:

Planning time – children decide what activity they will undertake in work time and share their plan with the adult.

Work time – the plans are carried out as activities within the classroom areas.

This includes a tidy-up time when children tidy up and return materials to their places.

Recall time – the third part of the 'plan, do, review' sequence when children review their activities with the adult and other children.

Milk time – self explanatory but may be combined with the recall time.

Small group time – usually consists of a specific activity planned and initiated by the member of staff but with children having some choice of materials and freedom in how to use them.

Outside time – again self explanatory, but staff to be actively involved, both physically and verbally.

Large group time – children and staff together for total group activity.

There is nothing magic about the order of these times and they can be varied. However, planning, work and recall must follow a consistent sequence.

The content of the curriculum is as important as its methods. The concept of key experiences is vitally important here – the fifty key experiences (described in chapter 5 and appendices) 'serve as guideposts for planning and evaluating developmentally valid programs for young children'.(3) Adults assess each child's abilities and plan to introduce key experiences according to his or her stage of development. There are materials and games for number concepts, spatial relations, representation, classification, seriation and time. Children learn these concepts through active exploration and experiment, then reflect on them through discussion with adults and peers.

The equipping of the classroom is also an important part of the curriculum. Each area should have a wide variety of materials with several things that perform the same basic functions, e.g. staples, glue, sticky tape for joining things together, and individual materials that can be used in a variety of ways. As well as toys and small items for representation there should also be a good selection of real objects, such as pots and pans, hammers and nails, etc. Materials are logically organised and clearly labelled so that as well as being readily available, their arrangement contributes to classification and seriation experiences.

Parental involvement has contributed much to the undoubted success of High/Scope. Emphasis is placed on parental involvement in the nursery, teacher visits to the home, and, above all, on the parents' role as educators. It may be that parental understanding, support and activity generated by home visits and greater rapport with teachers, contributed more than any other single aspect to the long-term success of the original High/Scope youngsters.

Chapter three

The school and the environment

The focus of this study is an inner-city school in a social priority area. It is approximately ninety years old and has on roll two hundred and six children plus thirty five nursery children. It shares the site with a separate junior school.

The total staff of the infant school comprises the head-teacher, deputy head-teacher, eight class teachers, one non-class based teacher and two auxiliaries. The nursery, which is part of the school, has one teacher (myself) and two nursery teachers.

The school is situated at the edge of a council estate. There are a number of problems in the area which affect the pupils. These include:

☐ a high incidence of criminal type involvement in the area, including vandalism and burglary – teachers' cars are broken into quite regularly;

☐ a high proportion of actual and suspected cases of non accidental injury to children;

☐ an extremely high unemployment level;

☐ many families are in need of support and are visited by social workers; the head teacher and staff are heavily involved in Social Services case conferences about children;

☐ many single parent families, many families with a variety of domestic problems and several fragmented families, which causes confusion for children;

☐ many children in the school have speech and language problems.

Many of the children find it difficult to adjust to the demands made by the shared experience of school life. A great deal of extra social training has to occur prior to and continually alongside other facets of education. Additionally, there is a wide range of special needs to be catered for, ranging from more able children to those with learning problems, and physical, behavioural and emotional problems.

All of these contributory factors have their effect on the children in the school and increase the problems faced by staff. It is the purpose of this study to show that however great the problems may be, early education can offer children identifiable long-term benefits if staff focus on the *child learning*.

Nursery education; the school and the status quo

My Local Education Authority has adopted a policy of community education, and its nursery curriculum policy states that: 'Nursery Education should be seen as a partnership between parents and professionals in order to aid the healthy development of each child.'

The High/Scope aim is also to build community links and extend parental involvement, so it seemed a very apt choice of curriculum.

The nursery has a policy of encouraging parental involvement and works to break down barriers; these may exist because of parents' own limited experience of school, poor self-image and wariness of the 'establishment'. Some parents display very anti-establishment/authority attitudes.

Gradually, over the last three years the nursery has tried to develop a more 'open' image. Various methods have been employed to bring parents into the nursery – parents join children on visits and outings, and participate in classroom activities, such as cooking and art. The long-term aim is to build the confidence of the parents so that they can participate as fully as they are able in their children's education.

Chapter four

Introducing planning

In the first year I began to change the layout of the nursery into specific activity areas and to implement slowly some of the daily routine recommended in the book *Young Children in Action* (published by High/Scope Press).

In the autumn term of the second year I decided to introduce staff meetings to familiarise the rest of the nursery staff with the most important parts of the daily routine, the process of planning, representing and evaluating by the children. This was to take place at milk time (about 10 a.m.) in each of our groups. We had divided the children into three equal groups so that each of us was responsible for eight or nine children at any one time. I asked the staff to question the children as to what they had been doing, where they had been working and with whom they had worked during the first hour of the morning.

After Christmas, I decided to concentrate on aspects of 'planning' as part of a small scale study for college. This meant presenting details to the nursery staff of why I wanted the children to plan their own activities and how I anticipated the 'planning' sessions as functioning. High/Scope quote in their manual that 'the aim of this particular curriculum was to foster the development and use of the child's intelligence'. Initiating and completing activities, and finding solutions to problems are regarded as vital to the child's development.

When a child does these things s/he deals with objects and events at his or her own level of intellectual development and assimilates information that is present in his or her immediate environment. *On their own*, they plan, build and combine ideas to suit the demands of the situation at hand; they accommodate their thoughts and actions to the objects and events they are working with. Through accommodation and assimilation, children take in and understand new information and it becomes part of their repertoire of known things. It becomes something they have learned.

Unfortunately I had an environment in which every event and activity was structured by someone other than the child, which provided very few opportunities for accommodative and assimilative learning. There was little chance for children to choose the objects they would work with, the events they would participate in and, most importantly, the goals which they would work towards. Much of what was taught was therefore never learned, and what was 'learned' was often quickly forgotten.

With this in mind, I wanted to create and maintain an environment which maximised the children's planning of their own activities and hence their accommodative and assimilative learning. This process of self-initiated action and independent work would give children both the freedom and structure they need to put their developing intelligence to use.

We decided to have 'planning time' at 9.10 a.m. each morning in our own areas with our groups of eight or nine children. The staff had discussed planning time; it was a time in which children decided what they were going to do, talked about the projects and activities they wished to engage in, and would decide what materials they would need and how to go about the work they had set for themselves.

The staff were provided with planning boards in order to collect data about the children's plans. We recorded these each day at the same time and in the same place. In this way we were able to monitor:

- if the children actually followed their plans;

- if they always planned to go to the same area;

- if they understood what constituted a plan;

- the child who did not want to make a plan;

- the child who said "I don't know what to do" or "I don't want to do anything".

We also thought about:

- how the children indicated their plans;

- how planning could be made more graphic for children;

- how adults responded in supporting each kind of planning;

- what the advantages/disadvantages of small group planning were;

- what the advantages/disadvantages of individual planning were;

- what would be the best for a particular child.

We began a regular staff meeting once a week with the head teacher present. We found this invaluable, as she often brought new light on problems and acted as a catalyst for new ideas.

Diary of events during the introduction of 'planning'

Week 1

The nursery nurses complained that the children were not tidying up after themselves, so the nursery was looking a mess. However, I had noticed that the nursery nurses were not supervising adequately, and allowing the children too much freedom to do as they liked instead of doing what was appropriate. I detected a note of rebellion amongst the staff at this point. They had been happy to introduce planning but were not flexible enough in their reactions to children's activities.

Their big worry was that if the children were allowed to use anything in the art/craft area then everything would end up in utter chaos. I pointed out that it would, if the staff themselves were not more vigilant than before, and saw that the children were taught to 'choose, play and put away'.

Because I had asked the staff to allow free choice of activity, they immediately took umbrage and thought that they were not allowed to help the children in any way. They sat and did virtually nothing for the first hour of the day. This was the time I had set to monitor the children's choices and to see that they were helped in every way to complete their chosen tasks.

Most children grasped the idea of planning straight away.

Week 2

As some children had difficulty in planning when they could not actually 'see' all that there was on offer in the nursery, the staff decided to change the furniture around so that all the areas were visible while the children planned their activities.

I also made a 'planning board' using photographs I had taken of the children working in areas around the nursery. With the use of these photographs, the children could see at a glance what sort of activity they could choose to do. This particularly helped the part-time children.

Sometimes children were disappointed when, having made their choice, they found that others had beaten them to it. If so, we suggested alternative plans: for instance, if the woodwork table was occupied we would suggest that a child made a model from some junk. This meant that only the materials changed so the child's original plan was not thwarted completely.

After two weeks we abandoned the idea of group planning and decided to ask the children individually on arrival what their plans were. We did this because we found that the majority of children preferred to begin 'playing' straightaway and were rather annoyed at being interrupted once they had started.

Week 3

We noticed that some of the resources were not being used so regularly now and that the children were opting for favourite and/or permanent activities such as sand, water and paint. We decided to use the neglected resources at another time of the day, called 'small group time' (which is meant to be teacher- initiated) and to reintroduce toys and materials which we hoped the children would remember to use during their own work-time each day.

The part-time children were now beginning to understand what a plan was but frequently didn't do what they said that they would do. The full-time children were beginning to tell their teacher when they changed plans, which was encouraging. As planning is a learned concept, I did not expect the children to understand the principles of decision-making overnight. Unfortunately, the other staff did, which led to frequent outbursts directed at the children if they dared to change their plan before executing it or without informing the staff.

Week 4

We realised that the children now needed more resources and materials if they were really to be able to make valid choices. With this in mind we again changed the nursery furniture and introduced three new areas. These were a junk-modelling area, a woodwork area and a music area, all of which became immediately very popular with the children.

The nursery nurses were quite shocked when I said that I wanted the children to have free access to the tape-recorder and they forecast that it would be broken within days. However, I took a chance that the children would handle the tape-recorder responsibly once they had been shown how it worked. This is indeed what happened.

Another question raised was that the children were not using the pencils regularly. As this is an important skill to learn we needed to find a way of encouraging their use. A quick glance at the shelves soon revealed that the pencils, chalks, crayons and felt tipped pens were all 'hidden' behind a large paper container and hence were out of sight and not very accessible. We immediately moved them to a more accessible spot and found that in a short space of time, pencils were again being used regularly.

This was also true of the clay. As soon as we made it 'visible' it was used more regularly.

Week 5

In order to facilitate the task of 'putting away' for the children, we labelled all the places where toys etc. should be placed. I discovered, to my surprise, that a lot of the children did not know the names of the toys– lego, mobilo, playplax – and perhaps I had been taking this for granted. Now I realise that when I have been suggesting toys for the children to play with, some of them have not known what I was talking about.

The staff and I have also realised that we use different names for some toys and different names for areas of the room. For instance I say 'House Corner', Lorraine says 'Wendy House' and Pam says 'Doll's House'. We decided to begin talking the same language, as this might be particularly confusing for the younger children.

Week 6

At the staff meeting we discussed a number of problems that had arisen during the previous six weeks:

Should each team member stay in an area throughout work time or move from area to area as needed?

Can a child go straight to an area without indicating a plan first?

Do the children need to tidy up before changing their plans?

What materials in particular work areas can be used in other parts of the room?

Do children have to tidy up just the things he or she used or continue until the whole room is tidied?

What if a child will not tidy up?

We agreed on the answers to most of these. Then one of the nursery nurses asked why the staff could not put out some of the toys on the work tables. The children, she argued, would still be making a choice after all and surely "the staff knew better than the children what they should be playing with". I had difficulty in explaining to the nursery nurses that I provided raw materials on the shelves, I did not put them out on the empty tables because I didn't want the children to have the 'menu' set out for them. It was very important for the work tables to be empty so that the children would be encouraged to choose what they really wanted to do in this time period.

Week 7

Following last week's discussion on what constitutes a 'choice' I explained that because the sand/water/paint were too difficult to move and carry around they had to be permanent features and therefore were 'out' for all of the time. This was not true for the rest of the resources. The staff are beginning to realise that after a child has made his/her decision then the adult can support and extend the child's original plan.

Another issue raised was that some children were making plans and then changing them on seeing a more interesting project. Was this wrong? The answer was 'not necessarily', because the whole point of planning was for the children to do what *they* wanted to do – so they may do themselves a favour by changing their plans for a more exciting and interesting alternative. "What, then, was the point of planning?" asked the staff.

I argued that when planning, the children were concentrating on the idea that they could be in control of their own learning. We are also stressing that they should choose what *they want* to do rather than what we would like them to do. As this concept takes time to learn we would have to understand that all children would learn at their own pace and for some it may take all year. We came to the conclusion that if we wanted divergent, creative thinkers who can make choices and be flexible in an 'open climate' then the children must be free to change their minds and not be condemned for it.

Week 8

We decided to remove the cupboard doors from the long low storage shelves and expected the worst. These shelves housed all the table toys and we wondered if it would result in a complete shambles. However, the children surprised us by putting things back in their appropriate places. With extra vigilance from the staff during these early days, we have found that patience does pay in the end.

Again 'planning' this week stimulated thoughts along a different line, which we explored at our weekly meeting. Were the children making the right choices, i.e. of more benefit 'educationally'? A question raised at another level was that the children appeared not to stay at their choices for any length of time. Reflecting on these points I had to go back to Piaget whose central theory was that children's thinking is qualitatively different from that of an adult and that children, given opportunities to investigate *their individual interests* will achieve more than being directed totally by an adult.

The question about concentration was also a complex one because a child whom you think to be working quietly on his or her task may, in reality, be one who sits still but does relatively little; whereas another who gives the impression of being a 'flitter', rushing here and there, could be a child who completes lots of tasks and may often complete them efficiently in a short space of time.

Reflections on introducing planning

We can see from simple observation how young children learn from 'taking the initiative' and 'producing effects upon the world' – children have an *interest* in what they are doing and therefore are fully involved in anticipating and solving problems. If we desire that children become intelligent problem solvers, it seems clear the best way to do so in school programmes is to give children plenty of opportunity to work on problems of interest to them – that is, problems that arise from their own attempts to comprehend the world.

Staff observations, taken over eleven weeks, have shown how quickly children respond to change and learn to take initiatives.

Over seventy five per cent of the nursery (25 children) have understood the curriculum component 'planning time', whilst twenty five per cent have not. There are several reasons why this may have happened; some of the children are young 'threes', are part-time, and demonstrated a lack of cognitive skills before this research began.

My personal observations have shown that the children in my group are using more varied resources and staying with their chosen activities for longer; social play has accelerated and is more extended than was previously the case.

We discovered to our surprise that even at an early age children could learn to 'choose, play, put away' and could also be trusted to behave responsibly with expensive equipment such as tape recorders and musical instruments.

As a nursery staff, we found that taking part in the research project had increased our personal effectiveness. The emphasis had been on learning from direct experience and although the intent was serious, we found the accomplishment of that aim quite invigorating and for the most part enjoyable. We took time to *reflect*, to take stock of ourselves and learn from experience. We found ways of looking at old experiences from new points of view, and of tackling situations with energy and effectiveness. Over a period of time, the depth and quality of our work relationships increased as we sought to develop our strengths and influence with each other.

We decided to develop and clarify goals for the future, and to explore more of the curriculum components found in the High/Scope programme which will be described in the following chapter.

As Bruner has rightly said: 'Change, when it occurs, most usually involves a better recognition by the teacher of what she is doing'.

Chapter five

Developments in the High/Scope curriculum during the 1970s

This chapter presents some of the High/Scope curriculum components which I planned to introduce in the later stages of my research. A fuller description of the key experiences, and ways of using the Child Assessment Records are provided in the appendices on pages 38 to 51.

The key experiences

The early 1970s saw a major step forward in the development of High/Scope with the introduction of the key experience concept, derived from developmental theory and the practical knowledge gained by the staff during a decade of work with young children. From the assumption that active learning is at the heart of the developmental process, and Piaget's theory of the most important cognitive characteristics of 'pre-operational' children, High/Scope derived approximately fifty key experiences to serve as guideposts for planning and evaluating developmentally valid programmes for young children. These key experiences should appear many times – they are not goals to 'attain' and check off but are more like vitamins and other nutrients whose repeated presence in many forms and in a wide variety of activities is important for good 'intellectual nutrition'. Key experiences are grouped under: active learning, using language, representing experiences and ideas, developing logical reasoning (classification, seriation and number concepts), and understanding time and space. (See appendix I.)

High/Scope believe that the key experiences will:

☐ guide in observing children;

☐ guide the questions staff ask, the problems staff pose and the way staff communicate with children;

☐ provide a tool that helps staff to see things from a child's perspective and learn about child development;

☐ assist staff in planning the day and specific activities;

☐ provide a resource for teacher-parent exchanges.

Observation and feedback

In the High/Scope curriculum, adults use the dynamic processes of observation and feedback on a daily basis – both in working with children and in training others to do so effectively. The processes are remarkably similar in either case.

Observation is a way of recording in words what a child says or does during a specific period of time, in as much objective detail as possible.

Feedback is the process of two or more adults talking about and analysing an observed situation to discover which opportunities for a child's growth and development are present, and to find ways to support and/or expand that development.

Ideally all adults involved with children take part in observation and feedback discussions. These discussions start with the adults who work with children on a daily basis and may extend to adults who are not as directly involved, for example, the head-teacher.

Observation and feedback discussions provide ongoing support for children and adults. Adults support children by looking closely at what they are doing, by sharing insights and understanding with them, and by generating ways to help children build on their strengths, interests and successes. Adults support each other by sharing their detailed observations of individual children and by designing strategies that will enable them to act on their own observations.

Observation and feedback discussions encourage teamwork – by teamwork we mean the close working relationship of all adults involved with any particular group of children. Adults who consistently observe, share and plan together will strengthen their ability to appreciate and support both children and peers. Because everyone in the team observes and gives feedback, everyone in the team builds both leadership and teamwork skills.

Observation and feedback discussions encourage adults to focus on the curriculum. The observation and feedback processes continually draw adults back to the curriculum to confirm their impression and ideas. As we have seen, the curriculum describes key learning experiences to look for in children's activities and principles to follow in order to support them. It provides a framework for observing children and designing subsequent support strategies.

Using the curriculum as the major reference point enables team members to make objective, detailed observations and to engage in feedback that is rich in dialogue, insight, ideas, creativity and usefulness.

Observations and feedback discussions in the High/Scope curriculum are guided by the same principles, regardless of who is doing the observing or participating in the feedback session.

Children are subjects of observation

For adults who work closely with children each day this principle probably seems obvious. Some adults using High/Scope may feel that observing adults rather than children would provide a stronger basis for improving staff teaching skills. However, Weikart et al have found that the best support for growth and development both in children and adults occurred by focusing observation on children.

Child observation not only tells us what staff need to know about children but also provides a basis for discussing the observed effects that we have on them and so contributes to a strong sense of teamwork among classroom adults.

Curriculum guides observation

The critical elements of the High/Scope curriculum – the ingredients of active learning, room arrangement principles, daily routine sequences and roles, the key experiences – focus the observations. The observer is therefore not overwhelmed by everything that is going on with every child at any given moment.

The curriculum breaks the whole temporarily into manageable parts. An observer might choose, for example, to focus on 'active learning at small-group time' or 'how Vicky and Emma used materials during work-time'. Yet the parts can be reassembled later to represent the whole picture of the opportunities for growth and development that occur within a particular childcare setting.

Observations record factual details

Writing down preserves situations so that the adult team can put them to good use. Writing frees adults from relying totally on memory to recall in detail situations they want to share and discuss. High/Scope's Child Assessment Record – the C.A.R. – is designed for this purpose.

Feedback is reciprocal

Effective feedback involves dialogue – talking, listening, giving and taking. Although the observer has the most complete set of factual, detailed notes, other team members often make important contributions because they can recall the same incident from a different point of view. Since such dialogue involves a spontaneous exchange of ideas, one can never be sure of what will happen during a feedback session. The outcome will depend on the contribution of each participant.

Feedback results in mutually agreed action

People participating in effective feedback sessions do three things:

1) Report and agree on children's actions 2) determine the extent to which children are engaged in active learning and key experiences and 3) decide which action to take next, guided by the curriculum framework. This last step is often the most difficult. Sometimes the observer has a predetermined idea of what needs to be done and tries to 'dictate' the idea to the rest of the group. Sometimes the only action necessary is 'more of the same'. Often, staff will refer to situations suggested in High/Scope curriculum materials in generating solutions.

In the best of situations, the staff agrees to try a number of new actions or strategies, some of which will work and some which will, after trial, be discarded. The point is to proceed through all three steps because each step – reporting, analysing, planning for action – is integral to effective feedback.

The Child Assessment Record

The C.A.R. is a simple form designed to help the teaching team record anecdotes of the children's development. It provides a systematic way of assessing a child's growth, and helps staff plan to meet the needs of the individual child and the group as a whole.

A written and dated record allows staff to see the children's progress and development over time, and helps the staff to remember the steps of their growth accurately. Completing the C.A.R. helps to develop the staff's objective observation skills. The C.A.R. is short and simple – only statements describing the child's actual behaviour are recorded. These vivid examples of children's behaviour are easier to share with others, such as members of a planning team, or parents, than are vague statements taken out of context.

The C.A.R. provides information essential for planning. Based on identifying what children do, staff can plan ways of supporting their development. Staff can see patterns of growth and development 'come to life' in the record, and similarities and differences in children's developmental levels become apparent. The C.A.R. also becomes a tool for learning about the key experiences. The more practice the staff have in deciding how to relate a child's behaviour to the appropriate key experiences and record it in those terms, the more comfortable they will become with that central aspect of the High/Scope curriculum.

Small group times

Some elements of what is meant by group time are very familiar to all primary teachers – an activity presented by the teacher in which a number of children participate for about thirty minutes. Group time in the High/Scope curriculum differs from the traditional 'lesson times' in that although teachers structure the activity, children are expected to contribute ideas, to develop the teacher's idea, or to solve problems presented by the teacher. Activities do not follow a prescribed sequence, but rather respond to children's needs, abilities and interests and to the teacher's goals. Interactions of all sorts are structured to engender quality experience – thoughtful interactions with objects, with other children and between children and teacher.

Small group times are designed for eight to twelve children working with one adult. A group time lasts twenty to thirty minutes and consists of an activity planned by a teacher/adult but allowing for individual choice and problem-solving by children. Small group times are planned to provide key experiences in language, mathematics, the relationship areas (classification, seriation, space, and time) and the content areas (art, drama, music, etc.).

Small group time provides opportunities to introduce the children to materials, concepts and processes. Adults provide new classroom materials for the children to explore, or new interest areas are added to the room. Group time is used for processes such as making cakes, vegetable printing and beading – activities which encourage the children to examine what they are doing. Equally important, group time allows teachers to assess children's abilities. Every adult needs some feedback on what children are learning. Small group times planned around specific experiences allow for observation of specific abilities. These observations can be documented on the Child Assessment Record and used for guiding a child's development.

The High/Scope team's approach to the curriculum is expressed in the following quotation:

> Initially many adults wish the curriculum framework gave more specific answers and directives, such as 'If a child builds a series of identical block towers then be sure to do A, B and C.' Instead the curriculum framework gives adults both a way to observe children's actions in relation to their intellectual development and a range of possible ways to interact with children in order to support and extend their interests and actions. Rather than give specific answers and directives, the framework gives *possibilities*, and makes the teaching team the curriculum developers. Knowing their unique group of three and four year-old's. they plan strategies and activities specifically for them.(1)

Chapter six

Introducing small group times and key experiences

In the third year of my research, small group time, and the concept of key experiences were introduced to the nursery. The intentions were to:

- [ ] identify the '50 key experiences', using the Child Assessment Record;

- [ ] learn to plan and conduct small group times based on the key experiences;

- [ ] focus on team teaching issues and strategies for working together effectively.

As well as using the Child Assessment Record, I also decided to keep a diary on a continuous basis, which would contain personal accounts of 'observations, feelings, reactions, interpretations, reflections, hunches, hypotheses and explanations.'[1] Accounts would not merely report the bald facts of a situation, but convey a feeling of what it was like to be there, participating in it.

Photographs of pupils working on specific tasks would be offered: photos would also show the physical layout of the nursery and whether pupils were working alone or in groups. Relevant episodes would be tape recorded, and linked with the photographs to describe what children were doing.

Initially, I intended to use unstructured interviews with the nursery nurses, and keep a written record of staff meetings. Later, when it became clearer about the sort of relevant information which was required, I could shift towards a semi-structured approach, allowing the staff to digress and raising their own topics as the interview progressed. All this 'evidence', the recordings, the Child Assessment Records, transcripts, diaries, notes, photographs, etc. would constitute the 'case data' for my research.[2]

The management and monitoring of the innovation

In October 1987, after all the new children had been admitted to the nursery, we began to implement the key experiences during small group time. There were two reasons why we began when we did – one of the nursery nurses was leaving in February 1988 to have a baby, and we had been allocated a nursery nurse in training from December 1987 to February 1988, which meant we would have extra help for two days a week.

However, the first five weeks of the innovation were ineffective for the following reasons:

- [ ] the nursery nurses were anxious about the new curriculum, particularly with the pressure of Christmas approaching;

- [ ] staff did not understand sections of the new curriculum;

- [ ] staff meetings were ineffective because evaluations were not recorded in a written form;

- [ ] a decision had been taken at this stage not to tape staff meetings because this posed a threat to the staff;

- [ ] some of the children had only been a few days in the nursery and it was thought to be premature to expect them to achieve or develop noticeable skills and concepts in so short a time.

Therefore I decided to re-introduce the curriculum innovation again in January 1988, and to give out detailed sheets about certain of the key experiences to familiarise staff with the concepts. Small group times were introduced on three mornings a week, for thirty minutes, during which time we would focus on a particular area of key experiences.

The whole staff began observation and feedback discussions at the beginning of each day. The day's activities were discussed and classified according to the key experiences, and we all began to understand the concepts more clearly as a result. However, we all felt that we would be more effective if notes were written about each specific group of key experiences (e.g. classification, seriation, number, etc.) and a new area introduced each week until they had all been discussed and understood. This was not intended to be a systematic attempt to teach key experiences or to memorise lists, but simply to clarify ideas so that we all understood what we were to be observing. We discovered very quickly that key experiences were happening all the time.

We therefore decided to introduce a different key experience each week, and everyone was given a precis of the appropriate key experience on Monday mornings. We then discussed how we could introduce topics related to that particular key experience during small group times that week. The staff were given an evaluation/planning sheet to help evaluate and write down their observations and ideas before and after small group times, and these would be discussed at the end of the week.

The intention was to cover seven out of the nine key experiences described in the High/Scope curriculum, as there were seven weeks of term during which this could be done. We chose: language, representation, classification, seriation, number and spatial relations.

In the first week we decided to introduce 'language' key experiences and to focus on these during the whole day, not only at small group times. We decided that staff would give priority to their own group's language data, but would also record other children's data and pass on quotes to the appropriate member of staff.

This co-operative approach helped staff to work together towards a common aim and consequently staff relationships improved.

The staff had come to realise that in order to monitor the innovation effectively both for themselves and for the children it was important to record their plans for small group times and to evaluate them regularly, preferably using a tape-recorder. Having overcome their resistance to meetings being taped, the Friday morning staff meeting was taped and this provided me with valuable information about their personal perspectives and how they were handling the implementation of the key experiences.

The Child Assessment Record sheets were now filled in regularly, and were used at the observation and feedback discussion. Indeed, they became the main tools for identifying and learning about the key experiences. Many helpful guidelines on how to approach the use of C.A.R. were found in High/Scope literature, and these are included in Appendix II on page.....

Using small group time

Our small group times were planned to last for about thirty minutes. Each of the three members of staff were asked to meet with their groups of children in different locations in the nursery at about ten o'clock. This meant that locations were changed every week on a three week cycle and meeting at ten o'clock ensured that the plan-do-review sequence which took place earlier was not effected.

Our location tended to influence our planning, as each venue offered varying resources as well as limitations. For instance, one location was the kitchen, another a small room off the nursery classroom, and the final location was the nursery classroom itself. We had to find new ways of using the resources available, as well as seeking to incorporate the key experiences.

The following are ideas that were used by staff members using 'time' key experiences:

☐ Cooking; making Angel Delight. Icing biscuits and making peppermint creams.

☐ Clapping; starting, stopping, fast and slow; walking fast and slow.

☐ Singing; fast and slow.

☐ Sand-timers; watching the one-minute timer and then the three-minute timer.

☐ Watching and timing the length of stories by observing the timers.

☐ Using the cooker-timer clock to alert children to the end of particular sessions (eg. end of work time). Shaking a tambourine to note the end of sessions.

☐ Use of a chart to show each day which member of the group was to help at milk-time and at lunch-time. By the end of the week most of the children understood the time sequence and could tell by looking at the movable arrow whose turn it was.

- ☐ Looking at real photographs of clocks; discussions about how clocks can tell us about when to get up, go to bed etc.
- ☐ Water play, sand play; fast and slow; speed of water and sand.
- ☐ Collage of winter-type pictures. Cutting, glueing, with lots of discussion about the 'time' of the year and seasonal changes.

During the period of the seven weeks' research small group times were organised and evaluated by all of the staff. Some curriculum areas were easier than others because of their familiarity – number, for example – but others like seriation, which were less familiar, evoked some anxiety but plenty of discussion. The staff all agreed that introducing key experiences meant rethinking their ideas about the content of small group times and this itself had been invaluable. Staff comments about small group times included statements such as:

> "I prepare small group time more when I know that I want to introduce specific key experiences."

> "If we didn't have small group time I don't think I would notice half that I am noticing."

> "I've liked small group time better because I've planned set activities. More thought has gone into my teaching."

We also noticed that using small group times helped to lessen sex-stereotyped behaviour, because staff encourage all the children to experiment with the resources on offer. Staff found too, that during these small group sessions they were talking more with children and observing needs and abilities in a much more concentrated way.

Staff views on the key experiences and using the Child Assessment Records.

The staff began to realise that mistakes were allowed and that if they learned from their mistakes then they were better teachers. For example, one of the staff chose bubble prints as an activity, expecting to be able to record good language observations. She quickly realised that no child could talk with a straw in his or her mouth and abandoned her observations.

Staff realised that they could help each other by sharing their ideas and experiences. One staff member said:

> "I think it takes years to get to know a curriculum really well. In a sense there are times when I am not relaxed now, too pressured to get observations down of one kind of another."

Another said:

> "I think when you stop worrying about what you should be doing and it becomes natural through experience, the more you do it, the easier it becomes."

Using the Child Assessment Record sheets helped to sustain communication between staff, as we had daily conversations about quotations by children. This enabled the staff to get to know the children (and the key experiences) in a more concentrated way.

The staff commented:

> "We find that we are much more involved with children."

> "Observations in the past were difficult because we were trying to generalise too much instead of focusing in on a set area."

> "The key experiences are always there and we know them. It's just bringing them to the front of your mind. We are looking and listening for them all the time. We are using the C.A.R.s to notice children who have been forgotten or missed."

> "It's good to have a focus for your observations."

> "We give children more attention when we are deliberately listening and looking for specific observations."

> "Observations are getting easier."

> "I think that using the C.A.R. has helped to organise our thinking into sections. I think that seeing it written down helps to see clearly where each observation needs to be recorded. If we had not used the C.A.R.s we would have been totally confused and we certainly would not have understood the key experiences as well as we did. I think that the innovation would have been unworkable without the C.A.R. It has certainly made it easier to introduce and to learn the key experiences."

The C.A.R. helped staff to identify their own needs for teaching and training. In reviewing C.A.R.s it was noticed that certain key experience areas were filled out more often or with a greater variety of entries than others. This pattern often indicated that the team needed to pay more attention to areas that were being overlooked. A lack of notes in one or more areas usually meant that some additional training in the key experience area would be beneficial to the staff. Based on what the children did, staff were now able to plan ways of supporting their development through the key experiences.

Articles about High/Scope appeared in Nursery World(3) and in Child Education(4) which helped staff to appreciate that there was interest in this curriculum and that they were not the only ones to take up the challenge of initiating a new curriculum. Staff members said:

"Although we had low expectations about the success of High/Scope, it got higher as the time went on. Higher than we imagined."

"I did not expect them to understand. It seemed a bit complicated. I mean, I thought it was complicated looking at it, never mind getting it through to the children. I thought we were expecting too much from them. However, you start to realise they know more than you think and they understand more than you think."

"The children are more independent now."

We discussed more about the children than ever before and criticism of staff by each other was virtually eliminated. After writing down quotes and observing specific behaviour every day about children, staff remarked:

"Our observational techniques and skills have shown a definite improvement and we now understand quotations from children in a far more meaningful way."

"The more you observe children, the more you realise how clever children are."

"I feel I know now exactly what they are capable of."

"It is now much more difficult to miss children."

"I think the children have got on better than I thought since High/Scope was introduced."

Another strategy employed during the research was the deliberate policy of opening up opportunities for staff to visit other nurseries using the High/Scope curriculum and to have other nursery staff visit us. A head-teacher, deputy head-teacher, a tutor from the local college, an H.M.I. and nursery teachers all came to our nursery to see aspects of High/Scope in operation. The nursery staff came back from a particular visit saying:

"We feel more confident about talking now about High/Scope than last year."

Comments from visitors included:

"It's good to see children organising themselves so well, and that they all know what to do at various tables without being told. They set the newspapers out if they want to glue, they know what they can use and are confident using it."

"How well the children work and with such concentration. No one is wandering around or sitting in a switched-off position."

"I have been aware of 'time' since coming into the nursery this morning. Having a focus for your observation really helps to channel your thinking and instructions."

Another visitor (a trained nurse) mentioned the labelled areas around the room, and said how helpful they had been to her in assessing the provision and resources in the nursery.

We had all agreed to try and keep the atmosphere relaxed and to enjoy the research instead of enduring it. Having a definite span of time for the research, seven weeks, helped to accomplish this.

Staff comments at the end of the research period were favourable.

They said:

> "The best way to present the curriculum sections was week by week and, yes, a week on each section was long enough."

> "We thought the twenty minutes staff meetings were long enough to say how we felt."

> "We are now feeling more relaxed and comfortable. We were not at first because it was new."

> "I think the innovation has worked well. I was thinking it was quite complicated and extra work but when I got down to it I haven't not enjoyed it. I have felt busy. I felt I was doing what I should be doing."

> "I'd like to continue this curriculum so long as we keep things relaxed"

Assessing the effects of the innovation

All nursery teachers accept the very real difficulties of working alone with a number of young children; team work adds another dimension to the job. As leader of a team, the nursery teacher is responsible for the development of voluntary and paid staff. She must ensure that they are well briefed and prepared, able to tackle their respective jobs, and that they receive all the necessary feedback to get satisfaction from that work. Unless the teacher takes this responsibility for her team, the nursery is unlikely to benefit from the shared expertise and energies of those adults. Certain management and inter-personal skills are necessary for the team leader, whatever the size of the team.

A team leader needs to support and direct staff if energy and momentum are to be maintained during the implementation of a new curriculum. She needs to have a clear vision of the goals of the curriculum, a hands-on management style of staying involved with staff, and a commitment to establishing high quality, developmentally appropriate experiences for young children.

When I first began to plan my research, I had to consider whether the new High/Scope curriculum was adequately grounded on what was currently known about facilitating child development and about what went into the development. I also had to satisfy myself of the High/Scope views on the development of adult competence in teaching children. Would there be continuous self-evaluation to determine programme effectiveness, good quality staff-child interaction and a staff unified and moving in a common direction towards the curriculum goals? Once I felt confident that we could handle these challenges, I began to introduce the first stage of the High/Scope curriculum into the nursery.

How effective has in-service school-based training proved so far in changing staff's priorities? Early in the programme I discovered that staff tended to continue doing what they knew they did best, and innovation was perceived as a threat. After some discussion and confrontation the staff realised the value of what they were being asked to do, began to believe in it and then to commit themselves wholeheartedly to its implementation. We all had to realise that change had to be perceived as a positive and necessary part of the job. That we have changed the way we work has been one of the most positive results of innovation, although we are all emphatic that much more work is still needed in order to have a balanced curriculum.

The priorities now are to give more time to helping the children to think ahead (planning) and to talk with the children more than before – individually, in pairs and in small groups. To do this, more time has been allocated to staff team planning, to evaluation of the curriculum (e.g. appraising results and changes using the Child Assessment Records) and to staff training and feedback sessions.

It is very difficult to say anything negative about the High/Scope innovation as it has worked so well for staff and children, with the greatest impact so far being made on myself as the teacher and researcher. We have noted particular improvements in the children's speech, language development, concentration span and, there has been a reduction in disruptive behaviour. The children appear to have more confidence, are more co-operative with one another and more independent, which we attribute to the High/Scope system of daily routine and 'open access' to materials and equipment. Overall this is an encouraging picture.

Since the introduction of the High/Scope curriculum, the nursery team have become more resourceful and capable. We know that we must co-operate closely, make decisions jointly, and determine a team approach to our methodology if the children in the nursery are to benefit most fully from our work.

Chapter seven

The future

Working with parents is the recommended final phase of the High/Scope curriculum and our intention is to extend the level of parental involvement during the coming year. The idea is to alert staff to the many ways in which parents can act as classroom resources and to provide strategies for supporting and encouraging parent/staff rapport. The following are suggested strategies for working with parents:

1 Home visits – during the summer term prior to the child's entry into the nursery in the autumn term – emphasising the fact that parents are the children's first teachers. Using the initial home visit to establish rapport and share information. Evaluate, record and follow up home visits; share with the rest of the teaching team.

2 Planning and participating in parent/staff meetings. Parent/staff meetings can be a valuable forum for the exchange of information and ideas and for mutual support if parents and staff jointly assume responsibility for planning, organising, selecting topics and leading the meetings. The more parents contribute, the more meaningful the meetings will be to them.

3 Learning about child development and classroom curriculum. All parents have concerns and questions about the nursery. What will my child learn? Why? How does the staff handle behaviour problems? How will nursery prepare my child for school? In order to help parents share their ideas and concerns, staff can provide information on child development at parent/staff meetings; they can encourage parents to observe and participate in the classroom to gain an understanding of the curriculum; they can discuss issues during home visits and at meetings with parent volunteers.

4 Contributing to the classroom programme. Encourage the parents to work as classroom volunteers. The following activities may involve parents working with small groups of children:

a) On a regular basis by:

☐ organising and running a book library;

☐ telling stories;

☐ helping with a particular art or craft activity;

☐ baking;

☐ sewing;

☐ taking small groups of children for language enrichment activities.

b) As appropriate by:

☐ supporting projects that arise by supplying artefacts, pictures, materials and information.

c) By making a specialist contribution, for example:

☐ a typist producing notices, newsletters, pieces of work for display;

☐ a nurse talking about her work;

☐ a pianist accompanying a group for singing;

d) By helping with routine activities, for example:

☐ *weekly* – sharpen pencils; mix paint/paste; wash paint/glue pots and brushes; check games, other equipment, rewind tapes; cut up paper; mount work;

☐ *monthly* – wash, mend, sew tabs on overalls; wash, mend, sew tabs on dressing-up clothes; update lists of catalogues, books, equipment; mend/re-label storage of language and maths materials;

☐ *special times* – accompany visits; help with sports day, Harvest, Christmas parties; help with jumble sales, school fairs; social evenings.

The research undertaken for the Plowden Committee (1967) showed that a large number of parents would like to know more about how their children learn in school, and also that parental attitudes to education accounted for more of the variation in school achievement than either home circumstances or factors in the school.

Where teachers do not have a high expectation of the parental role, there is a danger of a self-fulfilling prophecy. Parents who do not have a stake in their children's early education place a heavy responsibility on the nursery to succeed alone.[1]

References

Introduction
1. Pugh, De'ath & Wolfendale, 1984

Chapter one
1. Smith, 1908
2. Clark & Cheyne, 1979
3. Sylva, 1980
4. Berrueta-Clement, Schweinhart, Barnet, Epstein & Weikart,1984
5. Sylva & Smith, 1986
6. Tizard, 1984
7. Bruner, 1980
8. Stevenson, 1986

Chapter two
1. Hohmenn, Barnet, & Weikart, 1979: Hohmann 1983
2. Bruner, 1983
3. *Young Children in Action*

Chapter five
1. Hohmann, Barnet & Weikart, 1979

Chapter six
1. Kemmis & Alderman, 1981
2. Stenhouse
3. Tomlinson, 1988
4. Tomlinson, 1987

Chapter seven
1. Dowling, 1988

Bibliography

Almy, M., *The Early Childhood Educator at Work*, McGrawHill, New York, 1975

Baily, K.D., *Methods of Social Research*, Collier-MacMillan, London, 1976

Barrett, G., *Starting School*, (report commissioned by the Assistant Masters and Mistresses Association, 1976)

Bell J., Bush H, T., Fox, A., Goodey, J. & Goulding, S, *Conducting Small Scale Investigations in Educational Management*, Harper Education Series, 1984

Berrueta-Clement, R., Schweinhart, L.J., Barnett, W.S., Epstein, A.S. & Weikart, D.P., *Changed Lives: The Effects of The Perry Pre-School Program on Youths Through Age 19*, monographs of the High/Scope Press, No.8, Michigan, USA, 1984

Breedlove, C. & Schweinhart, J., *The Cost Effectiveness of High Quality Early Childhood Programmes.* (report prepared for the US Southern Governor's Conference) High/Scope Educational Research Foundation, Michigan, 1982

Brierley, J., A, *Human Birthright: Giving the Young Brain a Chance.* British Association for Early Childhood Education, London, 1984

Bruner, J., *Under Five in Britain.* Grant McIntyre, 1984

Clark, M.M. & Cheyne, W.M., *Studies in Pre-School Education*, Hodder and Stoughton, 1980

Cohen, L. & L. Manion, L., *Research Methods in Education*, Croom-Helm, 1980

Curtis, A., *A Curriculum For The Pre-School Child Learning to Learn*, National Foundation for Educational Research, Nelson, 1986

D.E.S., *Young Children with Special Educational needs*, H.M.S.O., London, 1986

Dowling, M., *Education 3 to 5: A Teacher's Handbook.* Paul Chapman Publishing Ltd. Education Series, 1988

Extensions vol. 1, no. 6, June 1987; vol. 2, no.2, October 1987 (newsletter of the High/Scope Curriculum)

Hohmann, M., *A Study Guide To Young Children in Action,* High/Scope Press Michigan, 1983

Hohmann, M., Banet, B. & Weikart, D. *Young Children In Action.* High/Scope Press, Michigan, 1979

Jowett, S. & Sylva, K., *'Does the Kind of PreSchool Matter? Educational Research,'* Vol. 28, No.1, p 2131

Kemmis, S. & Alderman, C., *'Towards a Science of the Singular,'* occasional publication no.1, p 4761, Centre for Applied Research in Education. University of East Anglia

Lalli, R. & Mainwaring, S., *The Daily Routine: Small Groups Times*, High/Scope Educational Research Foundation, Michigan, 1987

Moore, E. & Smith, T., *One Year On, High/Scope Report 2.* Dept. of Social and Administrative Studies, University of Oxford, published by VOLCUF, 1987

Oakes, G., High/Scope curriculum summary given at a meeting of Barnardo's Nursing Education Division, 1984

Pringle, K., *The Needs of Children*, Hutchinson, London, 1974

Pugh, G. & De'ath, E., *The Needs of Parents*, Practice and Policy in Parent Education, National Children's Bureau series, Macmillan, 1984

Schweinhart, L.J. & Weikart, D.P., *Young Children Grow Up:The Effects of the Perry PreSchool Program on Youth Through Age 15*, monographs of the High/Scope Educational Research Foundation no. 7, Michigan, 1980

Sharp, C. et al., *'Four Year Olds in School Policy and Practice.'* An National Foundation for Educational Research Seminar Report, July 1987

Stake, R., *Evaluating Educational Programmes; The Needs and Response*, (a collection of resource materials), Organisation for Economic Cooperation and Development, 1976

Stenhouse, L. *'Case Study and Case Records: Towards a Contemporary History of Education,'* British Educational Research Journal 4, no.2, p 21-39

Stevenson, C., *'The Young Four Year Old in Nursery and Infant Classes.'* Published for the National Foundation for Educational Research. Entitled 'Challenges and Constraints',1986

Smith, T., *Parents and Pre-School*, Grant McIntyre, 1980

Sylva, K. and others, *Child-Minding at Playgroup and Nursery School*, Grant McIntyre, 1980

Sylva,K., Smith, T. & Moors, E., *Monitoring the High/Scope Training Programme*, Dept. of Social and Administrative Studies, University of Oxford, published by VOLCUF, 1984-5

Tizard, T., Moretimore, J. & Burchell. B., *Involving Parents in Nursery and Infant School*, Grant McIntyre, London, 1981

Tizard, B., *PreSchool Education in Great Britain*, Grant McIntyre, 1974

Tomlinson, C., *Child Education on 'Play with a purpose'*, November 1987

Tomlinson, C., *Nursery World, 'High/Scope A Head Start?*, January 1988

Weikart D., Epstein, A., Schweinheart, L. & Bond, J.T., *The Ypsilanti PreSchool Curriculum Demonstration Project: PreSchool Years And Longitudinal Results*, published by High/Scope Press, 1978

Wolfendale, S., *'Parental Participation in Children's Development and Education.'* Partnership Paper no.1, National Children's Bureau, 1984

Appendix I

Key experiences

From the assumption that active learning is at the heart of the development process, and with the description from Piaget's theory of the most important cognitive characteristics of 'pre-operational children, we have derived approximately 50 key experiences to serve as guideposts for planning and evaluating developmentally valid programs for young children. *(Young Children in Action)*

Key experiences in active learning

Exploring actively with all the senses

Discovering relationships through direct experience

Manipulating, transforming and combining materials

Choosing materials, activities, and purposes

Acquiring skills with tools and equipment

Using the large muscles

Taking care of one's own needs

Key experiences in using language

Talking with others about personally meaningful experiences
Describing objects, events, and relationships
Expressing feelings in words
Having one's own spoken language written down by an adult and read back
Having fun with language: rhyming, making up stories, listening to poems and stories

Key experiences in representing experiences and ideas

Recognizing objects by sound, touch, taste and smell

Imitating actions

Relating pictures, photographs,and models to real places and things

Role playing, pretending

Making models out of clay, blocks, etc

Drawing and painting

Key experiences in developing logical reasoning

Classification

Investigating and labelling the attributes of things

Noticing and describing how things are the same and how they are different

Sorting and matching

Using and describing something in several different ways

Distinguishing between 'some' and 'all'

Holding more than one attribute in mind at a time (example: can you find something that is red and made of wood?)

Describing what characteristics something does not possess or what class it does not belong to

Seriation

Comparing: Which one is bigger (smaller), heavier (lighter), rougher (smoother), louder (softer), longer (shorter), taller (shorter), wider (narrower), sharper, darker, etc

Arranging several things in order along some dimension and describing the relationships (the longest one, the shortest one, etc.)

Number concepts

Comparing number and amount; more/less, same amount; more/fewer, same number

Comparing the number of items in two sets by matching them up in one-to-one correspondence (example; are there as many crackers as there are children?)

Enumerating (counting) objects, as well as counting by rote

Key experiences in understanding time and space

Spatial relations

Fitting things together and taking them apart

Rearranging a set of objects or one object in space (folding, twisting, stretching, stacking, tying) and observing the spatial transformations

Observing things and places from different spatial viewpoints

Experiencing and describing the positions of things in relation to each other (example; in the middle, on the side of, on, off, on top of, over, above)

Experiencing and describing the direction of movement of things and people (to, from, into, out of, toward, away from)

Experiencing and describing relative distances among things and locations (close, near, far, next, to, apart, together)

Experiencing and representing one's own body; how it is structured, what various body parts can do

Learning to locate things in the classroom, school, and neighbourhood

Interpreting representations of spatial relations in drawing and pictures

Distinguishing and describing shapes

Time

Planning and completing what one has planned

Describing and representing past events

Anticipating future events verbally and by making appropriate preparations

Starting and stopping an action on signal

Noticing, describing, and representing the order of events

Experiencing and describing different rates of movement

Using conventional time units when talking about past and future events (morning, yesterday, hour, etc.)

Comparing time periods (short, long, new, old, young, old, a little while, a long time)

Observing that clocks and calenders are used to mark the passage of time

Observing seasonal changes

Appendix II

Guidelines for staff using the Child Assessment Records

Nursery staff were given certain guidelines each week which helped to organise their thinking and behaviour as the innovation progressed. These were to:

1 Stop, look and listen before entering children's play.

Observing children was an important step in understanding, appreciating and supporting the learning opportunities in children's play. We began by asking ourselves "What is Vicky doing? What materials is she using? What is she doing with them? Is she saying anything that will give us a clue about her intentions?" Taking the time to find out unobtrusively all about Vicky's play was important, so that we could enter it or support it without disruption.

Having a C.A.R. for each child under consideration on a particular day helps to decide where each reported incident fits. Recording the incident in the C.A.R. also helps to translate our own note into a public form that is accessible to all team members.

For example:

Child Assessment Record

Child's name: Vicky

Language	Representation	Classification	Seriation
5/11 said "Is that the end of the story?"	6/11 Made cakes from pink play-dough with cherries on the top.	6/11 Sorted lego by colour and made individual towers using	4/11 Said, "I have the long-est hair in my class."

2 Take action.

The last part of any observation is to ask "So what?". Let us use the C.A.R. notes on Vicky as an example of what it means to answer this question. We know about Vicky's cake-making and appreciate her ability to represent. What can we do with this information? Here are just a few possible next steps.

As Vicky plans tomorrow, see if she can think of any other way to make cakes.

At recall time tomorrow have Vicky and the rest bring something they have used at work-time. See if they can think of how they can make cakes with their chosen material.

This initial step in the child observation process is often very difficult for adults because it means keeping quiet. Instead of talking and asking questions that might interfere with what Vicky is doing, we must quietly observe, refraining from making assumptions. At this moment, Vicky is teaching us. We must be attentive students if we are to be effective teachers.

3 Watch and listen playing with children.

Effective interactive teaching involves dialogue. For example, Vicky says something to you. By paying careful attention to what she is doing and saying, we can do or say something that 'fits' into her play or her particular line of thought. Watching and listening to children as we play with them makes being with children continually interesting because we never know what new insights are in store for us.

4 Record what we see and hear – it does not matter how.

Recording special events that we observe throughout the day forms the basis f effective feedback discussions.

Some adults keep a number of clipboards handy. The point is to use some kind notation to help staff reconstruct in as much detail as possible what we learned about Vicky, so that we can share it with other adults.

5 Share and interpret our observations.

As soon as we have the opportunity, we sit down with the other members of the team, gather notes together and discuss what was seen and heard. This is the 'raw data' – our next task was to figure out what it means. What do all the observations tell us about Vicky, Samantha and Caroline? How does what we observed relate to active learning and the key experiences?

In order to complete the C.A.R. satisfactorily staff followed these helpful suggestions from the High/Scope literature.

Always *date* the entries. Write them in language that helps staff remember what happened and allows others to understand it as well.

Make the C.A.R. part of the *daily* team planning and evaluation process. One member of the team can write down the observations shared by the group on that child's C.A.R. form, while another records the team's ideas of thing to do on the child's daily planning form.

Make entries on the C.A.R. at any time or in any place that is convenient. Do whatever works as long as it does not interfere with the children. Find a way to make entries as brief as possible so that you continue to learn and observe while remaining involved with the children.

Learn how to *select* which entries to make on the C.A.R. At first, the important thing will be to get the information down do not worry too much about which key experience area you decide to put it into, or whether you have already written about similar developmental episodes for that child.

As more practice is gained in filling in the C.A.R. it becomes easier to categorise events according to the key experiences and to be more selective about entering only *new* information. Similarly, it may become evident during a planning discussion that there is a need to focus more attention on a particular child and/or key experience. The ability to focus and to be comprehensive and/or selective as needed will come with increased time and practice using the C.A.R.

Appendix III

Observations taken from C.A.R. sheets

The following are examples of observations taken from the C.A.R. sheets for twelve children of similar age and background over the period of the research. These examples show how key experiences were occurring in all areas of the curriculum.

Language

Key Experience: Talking with others about personally meaningful experiences.

The following examples occurred mainly in small group time.

"I sleep in my own bed in Mammy's bedroom because my bedroom is being decorated."

"I've got my talking doll back from the hospital. Big Kerry pushed the mouth too hard and it stopped talking."

"You know what? My Tony's been to the doctors and he's got meningitis. I've been as well. I've got phlegm."

Key Experience: Describing objects, events and relations.

Whilst cutting and gluing old Christmas cards, during small group time, these comments from the children were made.

"It's got snow, people, birds, a house, trees. His feet is getting stuck in the snow."

Key Experience: Having fun with language; rhyming, making up stories, listenin to poems, singing and chanting.

After reading stories to the children in small group time these were their comments:

"He poured a teapot in his mouth."

"He stayed in for two weeks, then he burst out and he was a beautiful butterfly."

"She hasn't turned on the bedroom light."

"He's out of playschool ya' know."

Key Experience: Ask questions of adults and children.

During work time these questions were asked:

"My two boyfriends are painting. How can I marry two?"

"Who's taken dolly's dress off?"

"Is that a blackboard? I've got one of them."

Representation

Key Experience: Role playing, pretending.

The following comments were made throughout the day:

"I was the mammy and I cooked a pie and some soup."

"I made a car (in the bricks) and I drived in it."

"Fasten my coat (like a cape) I'm going to be batman. Da da da da da da da Batman."

"I'm the fireman, I put fires out."

While patting the dolls's back: "I'm getting the baby's wind up"

Key Experience: Making models out of clay blocks etc.

These observations usually occurred during work time or small group time:

Made a clay model with hair, eyes and mouth.

"Claire showed us how to build a big car [using large bricks].

We are putting in little bricks for petrol."

Key Experience: Drawing and painting.

Painted a picture of self with all features.

"I've done a walking stick and a Christmas tree and I've done white paint on my picture."

Classification

Key Experience: Investigating and labelling the attributes of things.

"There are three dogs, there's a black one."

"They're not stockings, they're tights."

Key Experience: Sorting and matching; noticing how things are the same and different.

Made a tower using red lego only.

Sorted Christmas cards into set of robins, snow scenes and animals.

Key Experience: Holding more than one attribute in mind at a time

"He was a big, fat caterpillar."

"Now all the animals are dead. (He then placed the toy farmer and horse upright.) The man and the horse are alive."

Key Experience: Describing what something does not possess, or what class it does not belong to.

"It's not raining outside."

"They aren't jeans, they're slacks."

Seriation

Key Experience: Comparing along one dimension; which is bigger/smaller, heavier/lighter, rougher/smoother, louder/softer etc.

Recognised smallest and biggest pieces of biscuit.

"All the boys have short hair."

Recognised the shortest and tallest children in the group.

"My sausage is the longest."

Recognised a little and a large book.

"I want a little glass of milk."

"I want a big scone and a big drink."

"Everybody but the boys have long hair. Haven't we all got long hair?" (Talking to the girls in her group).

Key Experience: Arranging several things in order or series; from the biggest to the smallest, from the heaviest to the lightest etc.

Fitted lids on to three different sized casserole dishes.

Made two lines of mosaic patterns and pointed correctly to the longest line.

"The castanets are the loudest."

Number

Key Experience: Discovering the relationship between number and amount; more, less, same, fewer, etc. ¯

"I've made a lot of dinners for Mrs Rose."

"I've got lots and lots and lots of snow in my garden."

"There's none more of these."

"I've got a lot of sausages."

Key Experience: Matching objects in a one-to-one correspondence

"We need five knives cos there's five people."

"I made one dinner for you and one dinner for Mrs Rose."

Key Experience: Counting objects and counting by rote.

"There are three cushions in this house."

"I've had two dinners."

Time

Key Experience: Anticipating future events either verbally, or by making appropriate preparations.

"You know what? I'm going on my holidays in the morning. I'm going to see the bonny lights with Brian in the car."

I'm going on holiday when it's very dark." (night flight)

"When my picture dries, I want to take it home."

Key Experience: Comparing time periods; short, long, new, old, a little while etc.

"It took a long time to make our party."

Key Experience: Using conventional time units to describe and represent the past, present, and future; hour, Monday, week, today, yesterday etc.

"Well, it's two minutes already, Mrs Rose."

"I played out yesterday with my aeroplane."

"It's morning, cos I waked up."

"It's winter cos it's snowing."

"I know when we are going to sing, in a couple of minutes."

Spatial relations

Key Experience: Experiencing and describing the position of things; in the middle, on the side, on, off, top etc.

Could put puppet in front, behind, at the side of, in the middle and between her legs.

"You have a cushion behind your back."

Recognised that David was in front of him, Michael was behind and Mark at his side.

Key Experience: Distinguishing and describing shapes. ⁻

"We need two square bricks to make a bed."

Appendix IV

Using the key experience to plan small group time

Spatial key experience – objectives

1 Walking, running, climbing, using large muscles, finding out what the body can do.

2 Observing and describing things from different viewpoints.

Provide materials and equipment for looking from different spatial viewpoints.

Teacher says before going outside "Let's see how many things you can do outside and what you can see when you move to new places."

Things adults did:

Focused on the parts of the body children were using to climb swing, run etc.

Asked children to describe what they could see when they were at the bottom/top of the slide, on top or underneath the climbing frame, in the middle of the tunnel, etc.

Encouraged children to guess what John could see from the top of the slide.

Observations

Cathy and Tara, on top of the slide telling others they looked little.

John had the idea of seeing the river from the top of the slide.

Rearranging objects in space

Provide large piece of coloured paper and a box lid full of leaves of different sizes and shapes for each child.

Have glue available for sticking.

Observations

Laura: Put leaves in rows, then in a circle (observed Tara).

49

Tracie: Made piles of leaves, large leaves on the bottom and smaller on top. All stems faced the same way.

Rita: First made circle. All stems in the middle. Forgot this arrangement and began adding leaves to empty spaces.

Eddie: Made collage. Intended to cover the whole space.

Tim: First classified leaves by putting maple leaves on top row, birch leaves on bottom. Then rearranged them all round the edges of the paper. In the middle he put leaves bent into tubes which he formed around his fingers and taped together.

Things adult did:

Observed children's actions.

Asked children to think of another way to arrange leaves.

Imitated Tara's circular pattern.

Labelled certain shapes 'row', 'circle', 'tube'.

Called attention to how Tim bent his leaf into a tube to help children become aware of other possibilities.

Ended with guessing game – the person whose leaves are put into piles can put his or her picture on this table and go outside. Asked children to describe their arrangement.

Described arrangements for those who couldn't themselves.

Appendix V

Using the key experiences for room arrangement

1 Fitting things together and taking them apart

Brick area   bricks, snap together railway tracks.

Table toys   lego, mobilo, sticklebricks, jigsaw puzzles, connecto-straws.

House area   jars and lids, mixing bowls with lids, clothes with snap buttons.

Art area   paint jars and lids, paste jars and lids, staples and stapler, felt tips and lids etc.

2 Observing things from different spatial viewpoints

Outside   ladder, slides, tunnels, seesaws, trampoline, climbing frames.

Inside   chairs, stools, benches, climbing frames, blocks etc.

3 Rearranging and reshaping objects in space

House area   dishes, shoes, dolls, teddy bears, pinecones, food, pillows, blankets, scarves, dolls clothes, towels and flannels etc.

Brick area   blocks, boards, pieces of carpet, cars, trucks, wooden furniture, cardboard boxes, animals, sheets and blankets.

Art area   scraps of material, paper of all kinds, paper tubes, magazines, leaves, branches, rubber bands, threads, string, elastic, paper clips, pipe cleaners, playdough, clay, straw, papier mache etc.

Quiet area   small and big lego, puzzles, shape sorter shapes, small tinker toys, gelboards, interlocking plastic squares, connecto-straws etc.